A LOOK UNDER THE HOOD

AVOIDING THE 10 MOST COMMON FINANCIAL POTHOLES

PAUL HOOD WITH CLAY CLARK

A Look Under the Hood: Avoiding the 10 Most Common Financial Potholes

ISBN

Clay Clark Publishing

Published by Clay Clark Publishing
1100 Suite #100 Riverwalk Terrace
Jenks, OK 74037

Clay Clark Publishing books may be purchased for educational, business or sales promotional use. For more information, please email the Special Markets Department at info@Thrive15.com.

CONTENTS:

....

I recently met the owner, Paul Hood, at a conference, and I was very impressed with him and his team. They have a whole life approach to finances and wealth building that I've never seen or heard before from a CPA. So, I called them up for a free consultation. Sarah, my advisor, was very helpful and knowledgeable, and gave me very clear direction on what would be best for my situation. I would highly recommend their services, based upon what I've experienced so far. They really seem to care about the long-term health and success of their clients!

....

Ideal Beauty Skin Clinic - -Misti Barnes

ABOUT
THE AUTHORS

Paul Hood
(Hood & Associates CPAs, PC)

Paul Hood Graduated from Oklahoma State University in 1989 top 1% of his class with BS in Accounting. He began his Career with the International CPA firm Deloitte and Touche as a Tax Professional and Employee Benefits Specialist. Began his own accounting practice in 1992 in Bartlesville, OK. Since 1992, he has acquired 18 accounting practices with offices currently in Bartlesville, Tulsa, Catoosa and Claremore. Entrepreneur at heart and has owned a bowling alley and sports bar restaurant as well as many millions of dollars of real estate. In response to clients needs not being remotely satisfied, became licensed to consult on Life Insurance, Annuities of all types, Financial Planning and Investments. He is recognized as a Personal Financial Specialist by American Institute of Certified Public Accountants, he serves on the Forbes Financial Council, and has been featured on radio, print, and television and an expert on tax and finantial matters. "We pride ourselves on being very Proactive in helping our clients steer their business or personal life to minimize tax liabilities, decrease expenses, increase revenue, pay themselves first and protect what they have created."

PAUL HOOD

"KEEP MORE, SAVE MORE, PROTECT MORE."

PAUL HOOD
(Hood & Associates CPAs, PC)

Hood CPAs took over our personal and business tax preparation because our previous accountant was bought out by Hood. Hood has been exception with the transition. And with that said, we couldn't be happier with the job this firm has done for us. Timely tax preparation with great communication go a long way. Customer Service is A++ and everyone has greeted us with a smile on their face!

Roe Creative Graphic Design - Tobie Munroe

"Paul and I teamed up to create this workbook to help you to get where you need to be and where you want to be financially. Most business owners earn large sums of money and spend even more. They find themselves perpetually behind with their taxes, behind with their bills, and dealing with CPAs that are reactive at best. We both believe that your accounting should be viewed as your financial dashboard and not your rear view mirror. However, nothing will change unless you do. Learning what to do is just half the battle. You must block out specific times in your schedule to tell

Clay Clark
(Former U.S. SBA Entrepreneur of the Year, member of the Forbes Business Coaches Council, host of the ThriveTimeShow.com and member of the Amazon.com best-seller's list)

your money where to go rather than wondering where it all went. You must change your financial routine to achieve your dreams."

CLAY CLARK
(Former U.S. SBA Entrepreneur of the Year, member of the Forbes Business Coaches Council, host of the 6x iTunes chart-topping ThriveTimeShow.com and podcast and member of the Amazon.com best-seller's list)

66

"You will never change your life until you change something you do daily. The secret of your success is found in your daily routine."

JOHN MAXWELL
Best-selling author of The 21 Irrefutable Laws of Leadership

The services offered by Hood and Associates are exactly what I was searching for. A proactive, entrepreneurial minded CPA team that wants me to reach my business AND personal goals. They offer proactive coaching services that provide business owners with support for goal setting, access to

Integrity Renovations - Jason Rau

YOUR ACCOUNTING MUST BE VIEWED AS YOUR FRONT DASHBOARD NOT YOUR REAR VIEW MIRROR

REAL TALK
WITH PAUL HOOD

"The numbers generated by your business both on the income side and expense side tell a story to those that are trained to read them. The vast majority of business owners as well as their accounting and financial advisors CHOOSE to read only the story of where they have been. Hence they are only looking in the rear view mirror of their business/financial vehicle. There is zero doubt that this process of only looking backwards is a major if not the primary reason for the huge business failure rates as stated by Eric Wagner of Forbes.

DEFINE. ACT. MEASURE. REFINE.

Nothing guarantees financial success but an essential part is to develop targets, budgets, and goals as measuring sticks to compare with actual results. Taking these PROACTIVE steps allows you to steer your business to avoid potholes that can and will destroy momentum and minimize success. There are three ways to be successful. (1)You can get lucky (like winning the lottery), (2) have some extraordinary, God-given talent, or (3) you can be deliberate in deciding to be successful and follow proven steps with proper coaching and advice.

FUN FACTS

63% Of Americans Don't Have Enough Savings To Cover A $500 Emergency.
Maggie McGrath
Forbes

100% of the non-homeless and non-cult member people I've met say they want to become successful.
Clay Clark

8 out of 10 entrepreneurs who start businesses fail within the first 18 months.
Eric Wagner
Forbes

Most of us do not qualify for (1) or (2) but the great news is there is a proven path to success IF YOU ARE WILLING TO WORK!

PAUL HOOD, CPA

REAL TALK
WITH PAUL HOOD

We are all constantly measuring things to create success. You use recipes to cook with, gas gauges in our car, a scale in your bathroom to weigh ourselves, and we look at the weather to determine what clothes to wear. Why not define and measure our key financial success indicators to help maximize profitability?

Fixed Costs generally are fairly straightforward to identify. Simply stated these costs are approximately the same month to month regardless of how much you work or whether you sell zero items or 1,000 items in an individuals finances and in the early stages of a business's life these costs represent the vast majority of expenses. Significant time should be spent trying to control these costs from the very beginning. Things like mortgage payments, car payments, rent and the items listed below are examples of fixed costs.

Fixed costs represent the bar you have to hit to break even in your business. The lower you can keep these expenses the faster you will become profitable. In other words profit starts to happen only after your net sales exceed your fixed costs.

Decisions to lease or buy equipment and office space, as well as administrative costs are major components of most company's Fixed Costs. While upgrading a home or are buying a new car are similar components for individuals.

PAUL HOOD, CPA

AMPLE EXAMPLES

 Internet   Heat & Air    Team Salaries   Office Space

 Insurance   Water    Printer Costs   Phone Bills

SUPER MOVE #2
VARIABLE EXPENSES PER TRANSACTION

REAL TALK WITH PAUL HOOD

Variable Costs, as they sound, go up and down in proportion to Sales in a business or income individually. If Sales increase Variable Costs, increase and visa versa. For individuals when we make more money we normally spend more on eating out etc. Businesses determine their gross profit per unit by the difference in Sales and Variable Costs like materials to make a product. This profit per unit allows Proactive business owners to determine the number of Sales they need to cover Fixed Costs (Break-Even Point) and then plan for profit increases as each sale is made over the Break-Even Point. If Variable Costs are measured and efforts made to continually stream line these expenses, less sales are needed to Break-Even and consequently real bottom line profit is much greater as Sales increase. By knowing your numbers you can measure how close you are to achieving the goals you have set. This all may sound complicated, so to make it more simple, if a company sells a product for $3 each (sale) that costs them $1 to make (variable costs), they have a gross profit of $2 per unit. If their fixed costs are $10,000 per month, they have to sell 5,000 units to break even. Their profit starts with the sale of unit number 5,001, therefore if you can keep fixed and variable cost down you make profit sooner.

PAUL HOOD, CPA

AMPLE EXAMPLES

 Pay Contractor Per Action Item

 Merit-Based Pay

 Cost of Goods Needed to Deliver a Service or Make a Product

 Advertising

 Savings

 Taxes

KNOW THE NUMBER OF CUSTOMERS YOU NEED PER MONTH TO BREAK-EVEN

REAL TALK WITH PAUL HOOD

"Break-Even is the initial Proactive measuring stick a company MUST know. It is calculated by dividing your Fixed Costs by the difference between your Sales Price and Variable Costs. Break-Even = Fixed Costs / (Sales Price - Variable Costs). Break-Even point represents the point at which your sales exactly cover your expenses. Break even in dollars is when your gross profit (sales less variable costs) equal your fixed costs. It represents the point where you have sold exactly the amount needed to cover your fixed costs. Up to Break-Even a company operates at a loss with profit occurring as sales grow from that point. Again, to simplify this thought, the point where you sell enough product that the money you keep after variable costs (costs to produce the product) pays your fixed costs (like rent and administrative costs) is your breakeven sales volume. Sales beyond this point result in profit. For individuals when your income equals your fixed and variable costs, you breakeven. Income beyond this point can go into savings or for luxury items. You have to take the time to identify your costs, classify them and monitor it all to know what sales or income that is needed to meet your goals.

PAUL HOOD, CPA

"Know your numbers' is a fundamental precept of business."

BILL GATES
(Co-founder of Microsoft)

BREAK EVEN = FIXED COST / (SALES PRICE − VARIABLE COSTS)

SUPER MOVE #4
TAX LIABILITIES

 **REAL TALK
WITH PAUL HOOD**

Taxes are a necessary evil but can be planned for and actually mitigated. Think of the IRS as a business partner when it comes to justifying things that can be deducted. Even though they are one that contributes very little to the success of your business they nevertheless are very interested in you being as profitable as possible. If we can argue an expenditure increases the long term profitability of your business we can take such expenses as deductions on the applicable tax return. Many accountants seem to actually work against businesses in this area. If it isn't specifically written in the Internal Revenue Code they think it is not a deduction. This simply is not the case.

Timing of when you or your business pays taxes is often a tool used to plan. Deferral of taxes to the future is simply trying to time deductions or income so you pay the government in a future tax year. This can be a good planning tool but really saves nothing but the time value of money. This method is the primary plan used by most businesses and frankly accountants but can actually lead to terrible advice when a company decides or is led to SPEND money just to save taxes. We NEVER recommend a company buy a piece of equipment, etc at year end purely to save taxes. If you go to a store and buy something just because it is 30% off you still are out the 70%. The theory is a company buys an asset on credit, gets the tax deduction in the current year but pays for the asset over the next several years. If you need such asset and plan on buying it in the next 12 to 18 months or want to upgrade equipment or a business vehicle to enjoy the lifestyle of working in your business, then great, but **NEVER SPEND MONEY JUST TO SAVE TAXES.**

One area that can be worth looking at is how to turn lifestyle into tax deduction. For instance if you desire to have land then research the financial vialability of having a ranch. With a profit intent and a resonable expectation of making a profit, you can deduct things like 4 wheelers, etc that are used in the ranch. A majority of the available tax deductions are for people that own their own business.

Entity planning and retirement fund planning are additional ways that can significantly affect the taxes that you are responsible to pay. The opportunities for such will be discussed a little later in this book.

PAUL HOOD, CPA

AMPLE EXAMPLES

 Payroll Tax (Medicare & Social Security)   State Taxes

 Income Tax On Your Salary   Sales Taxes

 Business Taxes   Double Tax Scenarios

SUPER MOVE #5
HIDDEN & OFTEN FORGOTTEN COSTS

REAL TALK
WITH PAUL HOOD

A large portion of our proactive time should be spent defining, measuring, comparing and adjusting the major expense items of your business as savings in these areas have the largest effect on bottom line profit. Attention, however, needs to be given to other less usual items that can have a large impact.

Theft whether from actual theft or from employees spending time doing personal tasks, playing games, or simply visiting in the break room can drastically affect bottom line numbers but the cost of such is often not measured on a financial statement. Employees can make or break a business's success and thus your hiring practices are extremely important. The hidden cost of hiring the wrong person for the job while hard to measure has a definite impact on productivity. Issues such as wasted training time, loss of customers from mistakes or errors, impact on other employees that have to cover for this employee's mistakes or lack of effort, drops in employee morale as well as actual costs such as increased unemployment taxes from staff turnover if not corrected can kill your business. Potential solutions include installing cameras, programs that track key strokes, recording calls, incentive based pay, production requirements and any other means to ensure you get a fair days work.

A major potential hidden cost in todays world is cyber attacks, unfortunately most of the time it is our employees that cause them by opening fake emails, not changing passwords, plugging in a flash drive without it being checked. Procedures for backups to protect your operations are critical. A trained IT person is vital. We have seen successful businesses brought to near closure from cyber attacks.

PAUL HOOD, CPA

AMPLE EXAMPLES

 Shrinkage Due to Theft   Worker's Compensation   Legal Bills

 Loss Due to Errors   Employee Inefficiencies & Turnover

KNOW THE NUMBER OF CUSTOMERS YOU NEED PER MONTH TO ACHIEVE YOUR DREAMS

REAL TALK WITH PAUL HOOD

The objective of all business should be the pursuit of a profit. The IRS actually creates a distinction between activities as being pursued for a profit intent and a hobby.

If your business intent is to pursue a profit, doesn't it make sense for you to be proactive and define the amount of profit you want to create? Once you define your long range profit goals we must break things down into yearly, monthly and even weekly goals. As a proactive business owner you have defined your Break-Even point and your subsequent profit per customer beyond Break-Even. The next step then is to take your profit goals and profit per customer calculations and quantify the number of customers needed to reach these long range and short range goals. Very few businesses even attempt to quantify these basic but extremely important numbers. The great news is that if you continue to be proactive these numbers often change as you grow and as you reduce costs or increase efficiencies.

The purposeof this process is to create a measuring template that can be looked at maybe as often as daily to make sure you are on course to reach your goal. If we calculate your average profit from a sale is $200 and your goal is to make $250,000 a year, you need 1,250 sales in a year or 105 per month. Knowing this allows you to have a measuring stick that is easily determined to see if you are on pace to reaching your goal.

Goals mean nothing unless they are specific and measurable. We encourage clients in order to have a balanced life to make goals for all areas of their life including faith, family, friendship, fitness, finances, and fun.

PAUL HOOD, CPA

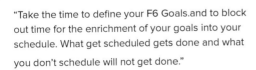

"Take the time to define your F6 Goals.and to block out time for the enrichment of your goals into your schedule. What get scheduled gets done and what you don't schedule will not get done."

CLAY CLARK
*(America's #1 business coach and the
former U.S. Small Business Administration Entrepreneure
of the Year.)*

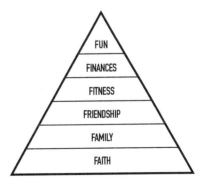

FUN
FINANCES
FITNESS
FRIENDSHIP
FAMILY
FAITH

KNOW YOUR PROFORMA

REAL TALK
WITH PAUL HOOD

Once you have defined your goals of profitability and calculated the number of customers needed to reach your goals, you have to monitor the results of your efforts both from an income and expense standpoint. Some call this budgeting others creating a proforma. They are indeed one and the same. Much like a personal trainer if you are trying to get into shape, a proforma or budget sets out your plan, gives you a measuring stick to compare to, and holds you accountable for the achievment of your plan of success. A proactive person creates line by line projected numbers on a monthly, annual, and multi year basis. You have to PLAN for what money you will bring in and where that money will go. The first item you should plan in the area of where your money should go is paying yourself. We are not talking about your salary or what you will live on. Pay yourself first means a plan to take a percentage of the revenue that comes in before expenses and set it aside for your future.

Retirement does not take age; it takes money. Retirement also does not mean you stop working and sit in a rocking chair on the porch to wait to die. If you pay yourself first you start creating funds to "buy back" your time. When you don't NEED to work to survive you are in total control of your time, which we all know is your most precious asset. There is a psychological effect at play in the difference between paying yourself first and waiting to save after expenses are paid. If you pay yourself first you never miss it. This is why 401(k) plans have become such a powerful tool for working people. If you pay all your bills with the intent of saving out of what is left, there never seems to be enough to save. There are always more expenses. The reality is we tend to consciously or unconsciously create more and more expenses to keep up with the revenue we create. We buy that new car or upgrade homes or give employees raises whether they deserve it or not. Pay yourself first and you will be amazed at how fast things accumulate through compound interest and dollar cost averaging (both discussed later).

The power of a proforma or budget is to proactively help you control your spending. For instance if you budget $200 a month for going to a movie and it is the 25th of the month and you have already spent $200, you wait till the rext month to go to another movie, without this control you always over spend.

PAUL HOOD, CPA

PAY YOURSELF FIRST

"Be the big pig at the trough."

DR. ROBERT ZOELLNER
(Thrive Time Show CEO and optometrist turned tycoon)

"Do not save what is left after spending, but spend what is left after saving."

WARREN BUFFETT
(An investor, and philanthropist worth over $70 billion)

SUPER MOVE #8
TAKE ACTION

REAL TALK
WITH PAUL HOOD

The most important thing you can do to take control of you and/or your business' future is take action. You must also recognize your strengths and weaknesses. You know the technical side of your business but how much do you really know about the accounting and tax side. The scariest thing is you don't know what you don't know. Investing in your business is much more than buying equipment. It is taking the time to work ON your business and not just in your business then hiring the experts to assist you in defining your key numbers, setting up monitoring procedures to compare these numbers against the proforma numbers needed to reach your goals. As well as holding yourself accountable to read your numbers not just looking back like a rear-view mirror but also forward like your dashboard on your road to success.

Your speed of success is not complicated but is not easy either. It requires a no-excuse attitude to deliberately do what it takes no matter what. It doesn't matter whether you are talking about finances, fitness, education, or any other areas of life. Be deliberate in defining goals, laying out your plan, executing your plan relentlessly, measure results around planned and refine your actions accordingly. Success in most things in life involve whether you have a team of specialists. Define your goals & desires and allow coaches and advisors to help design your plan based upon their experience. Use their experience instead of learning from your mistakes. These specialists should involve a business coach (HUGE if you want to accelerate reaching your goals), legal team, insurance specialists, investment advisors, and qualified proactive accounting and tax team.

Define where you are today financially including where your money is going. Detail out specifically and measurably where you want to go long term. Create a plan that takes your long term goals and breaks down action steps to get there. Measure actual results-VS needed results to adjust your course. You can be successful but it takes time and effort to measure and adjust.

PAUL HOOD, CPA

"A budget is telling your money where to go instead of wondering where it went."

DAVE RAMSEY

"Vision without execution is hallucination."

THOMAS EDISON

YOUR ACTION STEPS

Step 1
Find a Quality Accountant Who Has a Proactive Approach to Accounting, Insurance, and investing

Step 2
Find a Payroll Processing Company and Bookkeeper Who Has a Proactive Approach to Accounting

Step 3
You Must Schedule a Weekly Time to Meet with Your Bookkeeper

Step 4
You Must Schedule a Monthly Time to Meet with Your Accountant

Step 5
Cut 3% of Your Expenses

Step 6
Set Up a Budget

Step 7
Pay Yourself First

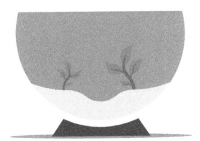

Excellent customer service . They take care of all my accounting needs so I can focus on working in my business and not worrying about the books . Thank you to everyone at Hood & Associates !

Beth's Pawfection Dog Grooming, LLC - Beth Strauss

POTENTIAL FINANCIAL POTHOLE #2

CASUALNESS CAUSES CASUALTIES

REAL TALK
WITH PAUL HOOD

"Besides your faith and family there is not much more important than the success of your business and or personal finances. You are blessed with abilities and the opportunity to live in a great country where you are allowed to pursue your dreams. How you use these God-given abilities is the greatest gift you can give him and your family. Hard work is often not enough. You have to work smart and have laser focus to maximize the effectiveness of your efforts. Success requires an attitude of short term pain that leads to long term gain. The major contributor to the high financial failure rate in America is the "I have to have it now" attitude that has poisoned our country.

Stop making excuses and begin embracing financial discipline. Losing or not ever having focus can set you back drastically on your path to success whether in business, getting in shape, or anything else you want to be successful at. Be the enemy of average and keep your eyes on the prize and have "pig-headed discipline and determination" (Chet Holmes in *The Ultimate Sales Machine*) to reach your goals."

Napolean Hill wrote in outwitting the Devil that failure in life is a direct link to what he calls drifting. Being casual and drifting in life, in relationships, in business, in physical fitness or in finances is a recipe for disaster. The problem is we are not taught how to be intentional. The primary focus of our professionals at HoodCPAs.com is to bridge that gap and teach business owners and individuals how to be intentional to keep more, save more and protect more of what they make.

PAUL HOOD, CPA

"Lazy hands make for poverty but diligent hands bring wealth."

PROVERBS 4:10

"Most people are perpetually locked in their present. Their decisions are influenced by the most immediate event; they easily become emotional and ascribe greater significance to a problem than it should have in reality!"

ROBERT GREENE
(Bestselling author of Mstery)

SUPER MOVE #1
TELL YOUR MONEY WHERE TO GO

REAL TALK
WITH PAUL HOOD

In life or business going along without purpose or defining where you want to go is a major cause of lack of success. You must be Proactive and define why you are in business, what you want to accomplish, when you want to accomplish it and how you plan on accomplishing it. You must budget both in your business and personally. If you are not deliberate in your actions and spending, your chances for success are very limited.

Let's say you decide to run a marathon (pretty awesome to put a 26.2 sticker on your car window). Do you think you will have much success if you are not very specific on training your body and mind? How many people can just mess around and go out and run 26.2 miles? It takes mapping out your activities over a 3 to 6 month time frame. Detailing out week by week activities to build up stamina to achieve the goal of completing the run. Treat your business and finances like training for a big event. Be laser focused and deliberate on what, when and how. No one achieves success accidentally. Success is intentional and well thought out.

The most common thing we hear from new clients is "I do not know where my money goes." The first step therefor is to answer this question by having them bring in twelve months of bank statements and credit card statements. With this data we have them catagorize all out flows and the results are always a suprise to them. They can't believe they spend that much on eating out or gas or late fees etc. This excercise is very eye opening for most people. Once we know where there money is going, we can establish where they want their money to go which gives rise to the budget or proforma.

PAUL HOOD, CPA

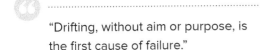

"Drifting, without aim or purpose, is
the first cause of failure."

NAPOLEON HILL

SUPER MOVE #2
STICK TO YOUR BUDGET

REAL TALK
WITH PAUL HOOD

Creating a plan for success physically, financially or in any other area of life is a great first step but remember Thomas Edison's quote "**Vision without execution is hallucination**". Once you define your budget which represents the details of your plan for success you have to monitor activities and spending and refuse to deviate. A Budget is designed to create conflict between what you want now and what you have PLANNED. If you always choose the wrong side of this conflict you are destroying your plan. You set yourself up to hold yourself accountable to be fiscally prudent and responsible. Remember short term pain equals long term gain. Delaying your gratification is the key to financial independence and success. Zig Ziglar once said, "If you will do today what others will not , you can do tomorrow what others can not."

Create a "system" to measure your financial activities. Set specific times and places to measure where your money has gone so far to allow you to hold yourself accountable to control your spending for the remainder of the period to stay within your budget. Creating a system to meaure is half the battle. Sticking to your budget is the other half. BE DELIBERATE!

When you are tempted to not stick to your budget remember that according to Forbes the average American can not put their hands on $500 to cover an unexpected expense. This is not because they have an income problem or are homeless. They have an allocation problem and do not control where their money goes. Plan, be deliberate and stick to your plan!

PAUL HOOD, CPA

"A budget is telling your money where to go instead of wondering where it went."

DAVE RAMSEY

COMMIT TO AUTOMATING YOUR SAVINGS

REAL TALK
WITH PAUL HOOD

Pay yourself first by creating an automatic savings plan based upon a percentage of your GROSS income not a portion of what is left over of the net. We have already established probably to no one's surprise that the average American is terrible at saving. We have become a society of "have to have it now" and spend what we make and sometimes more. We live in a society taught to get it now while you can and use all the debt you need. Our government leads the way as the teacher in this huge societal problem.

Psychologically, if you never touch it you will not spend it. If you automatically set aside funds before you start paying expenses you will build your lifestyle around the lesser amount. You can harness the power of compound interest and dollar cost averaging discussed later to magnify the effectiveness of your consistent saving. You must however have a financial planner that is independent from a captive brokerage house, bank, or insurance company.

It does not matter if you are debt free or have a lot of debt. Start saving now. By starting now regardless of your situation you retrain yourself to make different choices, you learn to live below what you make. Save first ten percent then pay bills and lifestyle with the rest. START NOW!

FUN FACT

54% had amassed little in savings—less than $25,000. Only 26% reported assets of $100,000 or more. Among the reasons for lack of savings, 40% cited daily expenses and 11% said they were paying off debt. As you might expect, having a retirement plan made a difference. More than two-thirds of those without a plan had less than $1,000 stashed away. Yet most workers say they need to accumulate $250,000 or more to retire comfortably.

Phillip Moeller
Reasons the Retirement Crisis Is Getting Worse for Average Americans

SUPER MOVE #4
DESIGN THE LONG-TERM LIFESTYLE YOU WANT OR BY DEFAULT YOU WON'T LIKE HOW YOU SPEND YOUR OLDER YEARS

REAL TALK WITH PAUL HOOD

Unless you think the government or your kids are going to take care of you, you have to be deliberate and Proactive in a plan to take care of yourself in the future. Your plan should involve what type of lifestyle you want and how much is it estimated to cost considering cost of living increases and estimating your life expectancy. These cost estimates then can be brought back to present dollars to estimate how much you need to be currently saving.

It is never too early to forcast what you will need to retire. Think of it this way; if you are shooting at a target that is 500 yards out, even a slight error will make you miss. If you move the target to 50 feet the same deviation will not make you miss. By forecasting out then bringing it back to present dollars we can effectively move a 500 yard target to 50 feet.

An independent financial advisor can assist you in these calculations and help develop a plan using a variety of financial vehicles. Proper planning necessitates an advisor that understands you go through two phases. First is the acumulation stage. This stage risk and volitility is our friend. You typically want investments that are growth oriented and go up and down in value. Through dollar cost averaging (discussed later) you can have success both in the up and down times. Second is the distribution time of life when you stop putting funds in volatility and risk are no longer your friend. We must transfer or mitigate risk in this phase of life. Once you define how you want to live and what it is going to take to get there, measure and adjust at least annually considering the need to rebalance investment holdings with the assistance of your advisor.

FUN FACT

Too frail to work, too poor to retire will become the "new normal" for many elderly Americans...The average 401(k) balance for 65 year olds estimated at $25,000 by independent experts – $100,000 if you believe the retirement planning industry - the decades many elders will spend in forced or elected "retirement" will be grim.

Edward Siedle

The Greatest Retirement Crisis in American History

Forbes

Amazing company to work with!! Paul and associates really know their stuff!! I always look forward to our meetings! #Proactive for the win!!

Team Next Level, Inc (Domino's) - Eddie Hall

AUTO-MATE YOUR SUCCESS

REAL TALK
WITH PAUL HOOD

Often even a successful business is not much more than an extremely busy JOB for the owner. Zig Ziglar once said that if your income is contingent upon you showing up you have big problems. You have to learn to go from Successful to Systematic. A truly successful business owner has utilized his business vehicle as a means to buy back his or her time to be able to have the freedom to enjoy life.

Most businesses start with the owner doing most everything. As success is generated, employees are added and the proceed of scaling begins. To truly be successful financially you have to leverage people, money and time. Once again we are not taught how to do this. We are all taught how to be a good technician, plumber, doctors, accountant, etc. Scaling your business requires you to focus more on using checklists and technology to create duplicatable processes to be able to get more done without you having to be the one doing it. Break jobs into tasks so that the lowest skilled person can do the task freeing up more skilled people to focus on their A and B level activities.

We have all heard that we need to take time to work on our business and not just in our business. Imagine if a professional football team coaching staff did not scout their opponents or evaluate their players or "game plan" to be successful. Don't you agree that such team's success is determined just as much or more by the planning as the practicing? To be proactive, you must plan your success. Success is not accidental. In this section we are focusing on YOUR success as the owner. Your business is there to benefit YOU and to help you accomplish your F6 goals for your faith, family, finances, friendship, fitness, and fun.

PAUL HOOD, CPA

CUT YOUR EXPENSES BY 3%

REAL TALK
WITH PAUL HOOD

The very first step in becoming Proactive is to do a deep dive into where your money is going. Make a list of your annual expenses from largest to smallest to be able to look for ways to streamline or cut expenses. The larger the expense the more room for improvement.

This deep dive should include evaluating bank loan payments based upon amount of payments, interest rates and payoff dates to consider consolidating or refinancing. Business Lease Payments often can be adjusted for items such as copiers. Payroll taxes paid on the owner are often an area that can be adjusted. Employee inefficiencies are a big area for cutting. Simple things like cell phones, utilities, shipping, internet, etc are additional areas cuts may be available. Some expense items tend to slowly creep up and go unnoticed.

Maybe consider cancelling your credit cards to get new ones to stop auto charges that you have lost control of or even pay attention to. Another area of fast savings is to evaluate the effectiveness of advertising dollars spent. Invest in advertising that grows your business.

PAUL HOOD, CPA

"Beware of little expense: a small leak will sink a great ship."

BENJAMIN FRANKLIN

"Too many people spend money they earned... To buy things they don't want... to impress people that they don't like."

WILL ROGERS

SUPER MOVE #2
INCREASE YOUR INCOME BY 3%

REAL TALK
WITH PAUL HOOD

Increasing your income generally is not as hard as most businesses make it. A good business coach can assist you with marketing efforts to increase customer traffic. The best advice you can get is be proud of your product or service offering and do not be afraid to raise your prices. Give a little more service if you need to feel justified but your sales price should be increased annually at a minimum.

Employees expect raises, utility bills increase, cost of materials, advertising, and almost every other expense increase annually. The average cost of living increase is generally about 2% by itself. If you go years without increasing your sales price and continually absorb the increases in costs your profit margin will shrink to nothing eventually.

If you are an employee, stop giving the government an interest free loan through having extra taken out of your paycheck then getting a large refund at the end of the year. This is simply lazy planning and people tend to blow there refunds when they get them. Put the excess in real savings and leave it alone. You are already used to not living on it. Stop giving it to Uncle Sam and start saving for your future.

MARINATION MOMENT

How different would the world be without Thomas Edison's inventions?

You always want to provide a fair service or product for a fair price to the consumer. Price gouging will eventually lead to someone else entering your market and taking your business. Most of the time your pricing structure is extremely far from price gouging so get to increasing your sales price. Just increasing your prices accross the board by 3% can make a huge difference.

PAUL HOOD, CPA

"Opportunity is missed by most people because it is dressed in overalls and looks like work."

THOMAS EDISON
(An American inventor and businessman, who has been described as America's greatest inventor. He developed many devices that greatly influenced life around the world including the first modern motion picture camera, the first recorded audio and the first practical electric light bulb)

"Work like hell. I mean you just have to put in 80 to 100 hour weeks every week. [This] improves the odds of success. If other people are putting in 40 hour work weeks and you're putting in 100 hour work weeks, then even if you're doing the same thing you know that you will achieve in 4 months what it takes them a year to achieve."

ELON MUSK
(Musk is the founder, CEO, and CTO of SpaceX; a co-founder, a Series A investor, CEO, and product architect of Tesla Inc.; Co-chairman of OpenAI; founder and CEO of Neuralink. He was previously co-founder and chairman of SolarCity; co-founder of Zip2; and founder of X.com, which merged with Confinity and took the name PayPal.)

SUPER MOVE #3
COMMIT TO AUTOMATICALLY INVESTING 3% OF YOUR GROSS REVENUE

 ### REAL TALK
WITH PAUL HOOD

Successful people are always people that understand delayed gratification. Effort today means results tomorrow. Imagine a farmer that sows seed today and gains his harvest months later. The key to this Super Move is to SAVE BEFORE YOU SPEND! Very few people have money left over at the end of the month after paying bills. If you pay yourself first by saving a minimum of 3% of gross business income or 10% percent of wages or net income you will naturally adjust your expenses in kind. There is a strange voodoo or psychological or maybe even subconscious process that happens.

As previously discussed when you are in the accumulation phase of life, you can harness principles of dollar cost averaging (discussed later) to almost guarantee success in saving. If the market is high when you save yay but if it is low when you save double yay because you are buying it on sale. It doesn't matter your current or financial position, save now!

You absolutely have to carve off funds created by your business to set aside to begin "buying back" your time in the future. If you constantly "eat all that you kill" one day you will starve because you will not be able to hunt. Time can absolutely be in your favor or massively against you. The Bible says in Proverbs 21:20 "The wise man saves for the future, but the foolish man spends whatever he gets." Be proactive and save first.

PAUL HOOD, CPA

"Financial peace isn't the acquisition of stuff. It's learning to live on less than you make, so you can give money back and have money to invest. You can't win until you do this."

DAVE RAMSEY
(National talk radio host and a New York Times best-selling author)

COMPOUND INTEREST WORKS HARDER THAN YOU DO

REAL TALK WITH PAUL HOOD

Do you know what a cartoon minion is? Those little yellow dudes that run around working like crazy. Where you save or invest you are creating minions. These minions (your money) go to work and making more minions (Interest and earnings.) When you have enough minions you have the choice of not working any longer. They allow you to buy back your time.

You should get paid and rewarded for your efforts and sacrifice. People and institutions will pay you to use the funds you save because you delay your gratification. Banks pay you for being a good steward and charge others for being foolish. Compound interest is a powerful thing for you or against you depending on which side of the equation you are on.

By paying yourself first through saving a percentage of the gross income, you set yourself on a path that your money works when you work and when you eat and when you sleep and when you are on vacation. You earn interest on your savings then you earn interest on the interest you earned. We all know the destructive power that credit card debt has on individuals. This destructive power is the exact same power that you can harness for good for yourself. The sooner you start saving and paying yourself first the faster you see substantial results.

PAUL HOOD, CPA

"Compound interest is the eighth wonder of the world. He who understands it, earns it... He who doesn't... Pays it."

ALBERT EINSTEIN
(A German born-theoretical physicist responsible for convincing President Roosevelt that America must be the first to create an atomic weapon to defeat the Germans and the Japanese in World War II)

AMPLE EXAMPLE:
DOW JONES 1989 VS. NOW

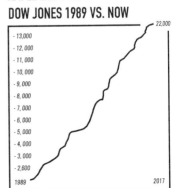

SUPER MOVE #5
USE THE POWER OF DOLLAR COST AVERAGING

 **REAL TALK WITH PAUL HOOD**

While compound interest is simply being paid for the use of your money, Dollar Cost Averaging is a method to mitigate downside risk in investments that are volatile and go up and down in price. For example let's say a person wants to invest $1,000 per month into a stock. In month one, the stock is selling for $1,000 per share so the investor was able to buy one share. After 30 days this particular stock dropped 50% and is now worth $500. Notice that the investment went down 50% ($1,000 to $500) but to get back to even it has to go up 100% ($500 to $1,000) . What most investors do not realize is the downside has double the impact as the upside. If the investor invests another $1,000 as planned they purchased two shares this time for a total cost basis of $2,000 and owning 3 shares. Their average cost basis is now $667 per share ($2,000 divided by 3 shares). The power of this is now the stock only has to go up from $500 per share to $667 for the investor to be back to even instead of $500 to $1,000.

Dollar Cost Averaging helps the investor take advantage of the down times in investing. This principle is a major reason people are more successful through their 401(k). With a 401(k) employees pay themselves FIRST.

When you are in the accumulation phase of life you want to take advantage of volatility. If the market is up your values are up. If the market is down you get to buy things on sale. We call this the automatic millionaire plan. It is extremely important you work with professionals that know what they are doing and are independent from any financial firm. Preferrably one that is considered a fiducary for you. We want to make sure they work 100% for your best interest and not for those of their employer.

PAUL HOOD, CPA

DEFINITION MAGICIAN

Dollar-cost averaging (DCA) is an investment technique of buying a fixed dollar amount of a particular investment on a regular schedule, regardless of the share price. The investor purchases more shares when prices are low and fewer shares when prices are high. The premise is that DCA lowers the average share cost over time, increasing the opportunity to profit. The DCA technique does not guarantee that an investor won't lose money on investments. Rather, it is meant to allow investment over time instead of investment as a lump sum.
Edward Siedle

"Never depend on a single income. Make investments to create a second source."

WARREN BUFFETT
(The founder of Berkshire Hathaway and one of the most successful investors in the world.)

"Be greedy when others are fearful and fearful when others are greedy."

WARREN BUFFETT
(The founder of Berkshire Hathaway and one of the most successful investors in the world.)

Love the full package of services of business and personal, bookkeeping, payroll, tax and help with finances

Tip Top K9 - Ryan & Rachel Wimpey

DEVELOP CLEAR GOALS FOR YOUR FINANCIAL FUTURE

REAL TALK
WITH PAUL HOOD

If you don't define where you want to go how will you know if you get there or even how to get there? How will you know if you are on track or need to change directions? Obviously without defining very specifically and clearly your financial goals you can not design a Proactive step by step plan. Without a plan you can't be Proactive and will likely not be successful. Define, execute, measure, and refine your plan and your chances for success are greatly enhanced.

Successful people almost always predetermine where they want to go but most people spend more time planning a vacation or a wedding than they plan their financial future. Pastor Craig Groeschel said "Victory isn't always what you conquer in the future, victory is staying faithful and obedient today." This principle applies to all aspects of life including financial. If you set very clear long term goals then create a plan to reach those goals that incude short term goals that build upon each other, you create a series of measuring points to keep you on track. The war is won by winning the daily battles but how do you know if you won the battle if you do not define what victory is? If you needed to get 30 new customers a month, daily victory is getting a new customer a day!

PAUL HOOD, CPA

SET SMART GOALS TO ACHIEVE SUCCESS

S PECIFIC

M EASUREABLE

A ACTIONABLE

R EALISTIC

T IMELY

SUPER MOVE #1
DETERMINE YOUR F6 LIFESTYLE GOALS

REAL TALK WITH PAUL HOOD

A happy life is a balanced life. We all have our dream life swimming around in our minds and hearts some place. Most do not clearly define on paper their ideal life. The same principles of success and proactivity apply to faith, family, friends, fitness, and fun. SCHEDULE time for the important things in life in addition to work and business. As "they" say, all work and no play is not a good or healthy thing.

I am not talking figuratively, I mean literally right now write down two or three goals for each of the F6 goals. Have you every heard if you are in a car you steer towards what you are looking at? For instance, if you are going off the road headed for a tree, look away from the tree. If you focus on the tree you will hit the tree. Plan for this life and steer yourself in the direction to create that life.

PAUL HOOD, CPA

"Begin with the end in mind."

STEPHEN COVEY
(The best-selling author of The 7 Habits of HIghly Effective People)

FUN FACT

1 in 3 Americans have no retirement savings.
Time Magazine

63% of Americans Don't Have Enough to Cover a $500 Emergency.
Forbes

ESTABLISH YOUR F6 GOALS

Faith Goals

Family Goals

Friendship Goals

Fitness Goals

Financial Goals

Fun Goals

UPER MOVE #2
AKE SPECIFIC
OALS

REAL TALK
WITH PAUL HOOD

goal is not a goal if it is not specific. It is a wish or a hope. "I want to be financially
ndependent," for example, cannot be quantified and as such can not be measured
gainst a plan. In order to execute, measure, and then refine your plan it first must
e DEFINED. A better goal would be to have an income stream not dependent upon
ou working of $100,000 per year. This goal is specifically defined, can be broken
own into the funds you need to have set aside which can be segmented into monthly
eposits into investments and then measured for success on a quarterly and annual
asis. The same steps and principles for measuring financial / savings goals apply for
he rest of your F6 goals. Establish a specific time and location that you will measure
he progress verses what needs to happen to reach your goals.

et your calender out and preplan by putting in when and where you are going to
xercise, go over your accounting, take your spouse on a date, hang out with friends
tc. Plan your daily life like you would a vacation. Know where you need to be, when
ou need to be there, who else needs to be with you and what item you need to
omplete the preplanned task. Your best decisions got you to where you are right now.
f you want things to be different, define what different is. Don't say I want to be in
hape. Say I want to weigh 165 by June 1st. This specific goal allows you to go further
nd say to reach my goal I need to loose one pound a week for the next fifteen weeks.
y being specific you can track whether you are on pace or ahead or behind which
llows you to adjust your efforts.

AUL HOOD, CPA

"If you want to be happy, set a goal that commands your thoughts,
liberates your energy and inspires your hopes."

ANDREW CARNEGIE

SUPER MOVE #3
MAKE MEASURABLE GOALS

REAL TALK
WITH PAUL HOOD

Once specific goals are defined, the process of measuring and adjusting starts. If the goal relates to investing, a good independent financial advisor will actually use "Goals Based Investing" in designing your recommended portfolio. A separate portfolio of investments should be established for different goals. For instance you may have goals to buy a new house, set money aside for kids or grandkids college and retirement. A separate portfolio is necessary because there are different timelines and therefore different volatility factors. The advisor's software will track your actual results at any given time against the plan laid out to reach your goals. The purpose for measuring actual v. planned is to make adjustments to keep actual at or above planned.

These goals should be set for all areas of life. How many books are you going to read? How much time are you going to spend with family and friends? When do you want to retire or be able to "buy back" your time? What physical shape do you want to be in? What type of house or other tangible assets do you want?

A similar process as "Goals Based Investing" should be used with your fitness, your business and other F6 areas of life. Have a goal to grow your business, to cut costs, to increase productivity, and enhance quality. If you can not measure your progress you do not have a true goal. It takes time to establish measurable goals but the results will suprise you. Measure goals and progress in dollars, or units, or hours spent, or calls made, or steps taken. How many of us own a Fitbit or similar device?

A Fitbit is really of no use unless you first establish the measurable goal to take 10,000 steps. I know people that literally freak out if they forget to weat theirs "they are wasting steps." The reality is those steps are not being measured and tracked. Create a "Fitbit" mentality for your finances and see how your success is magnified because you will not stop your day until you have reached your step, goal, or number of calls or widgets made, etc.

PAUL HOOD, CPA

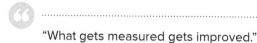

"What gets measured gets improved."

PETER DRUCKER

SUPER MOVE #4
MAKE ACTIONABLE GOALS

REAL TALK
WITH PAUL HOOD

With specific goals defined and measuring procedures in place action must be taken when actual and planned results get off. By converting long term goals into short term steps to achieve your goal, you are creating the ability to take action to adjust the direction of the plan. The longer the time horizon for the measurable steps the less opportunity there is to make changes. An actionable plan is one with a minimum of quarterly evaluations and comparisons of planned results and actual results. Imagine going on a trip from Oklahoma to California and your map view is a 1,000 mile view. The best you can do is steer your car west and head out. The tighter the map the more specific your planned trip and the better the chance of you getting where you are going.

In addition when you actually have a plan there is less of a chance for unknown road blocks or trouble. If you have a detailed budget for instance, you are telling your money where to go, you are preplanning in detail your money outflows and are therefore less apt to make impulse purchases that do not fit into your plan. Or if you are on a specific plan to get into shape and you preplanned your meals, you are less apt to stop and eat that triple cheeseburger you just heard about on the radio.

PAUL HOOD, CPA

"Successful people maintain a positive focus in life no matter what is going on around them. They stay focused on their past successes rather than their past failures, and on the next action steps they need to take to get them closer to the fulfillment of their goals rather than all the other distractions that life presents to them."

JACK CANFIELD

SUPER MOVE #5
MAKE REALISTIC GOALS

REAL TALK
WITH PAUL HOOD

Unrealistic goals are not goals at all but fantasy and only serve to create frustration which leads to quitting on the process. A goal to have 10 million dollars at 65 when you are 55 and make $100,000 a year probably isn't realistic unless you are real lucky at the lottery. Goals that stretch you and force you to dream big however are not necessarily unrealistic. The determining factor as to whether a goal is realistic really boils down to whether the steps necessary to attain the goal are realistic. Dream big then break down the plan that would have to be put in place to achieve that goal. Seek advice from a qualified business coach and a proactive Accountant to work the numbers and analyze the plan. What you absolutely do not do is ask your neighbors or family or friends what they think. There is a story told by men who catch crabs for a living that if you have one crab in a basket you have to put a lid on it. If you have more than one crab in the basket you don't need a lid because every time one tries to climb out another one will reach up and pull him down.

Realistic goals do not mean easy goals. Set that goal high than back into the short term results it will take to achieve that goal. Sometimes to make an unrealistic goal work you merely have to extend the time to get there. For instance if your goal requires you to add fifty new clients a month and you determine that is not realistic then push the time it takes out to hit the goal so that it takes 25 new clients a month to reach it.

PAUL HOOD, CPA

"You need to overcome the tug of people against you as you reach for high goals."

GEORGE S. PATTON
(US General who served in World War II)

UPER MOVE #6
1AKE TIMELY
50ALS

REAL TALK
WITH PAUL HOOD

/e all make time for what is important to us. If your goals are real and you are rious about reaching them you will make time to clearly define, take action, ieasure results and refine the steps as necessary. If your goal is to be a millionaire id the only possible way of that happening is to win the lottery, but you do not even ke the time to buy a ticket, you are not serious about even this unrealistic goal. You id only you are responsible for attaining your goals. Take responsibility for your nancial future because if you do not achieve your goals it is your fault and yours one. It is not the government's fault or because the economy is bad or any other xcuse you can come up with. Reactive people make excuses and believe they are ictims. Things happen to them instead of them making things happen. A Proactive erson takes responsibility, plans, schedules, measures and adjusts on their path to ie success as THEY have defined it.

he time frame needed to reach your goals is important as well. If the goal is too far i the future you have more of a tendency to drift, make excuses and procrastinate. et those long term goals then set interim goals that are more timely and able to e measured but that stack on top of each other with the long term goal in mind. tacking shorter term goals that build up to your bigger long term goal will help keep our daily motivation going.

AUL HOOD, CPA

heck Your List

- [ ] Defined Place to Do Your Accounting
- [ ] Defined Time to Do Your Accounting
- [ ] Defined Budget
- [ ] Create Deadlines
- [ ] Defined Time to Meet with Your Accountant at Least Once Per Quarter
- [ ] Find an Accountant That Can Be Proactive

"Discipline is the bridge between goals and accomplishment."

JIM ROHN

"What gets scheduled gets done."

LEE COCKERELL

Worked with Hood & Associates for 15 years. The words I would use to describe them are Consistent, Knowledgeable, responsive. They have been very supportive in helping with our success and have always given us confidince in what they bring.

Tate Boys Tires, LLC – Marty Schoenthaler

LEARNING HOW TO READ YOUR FINANCIAL DASHBOARD

REAL TALK WITH PAUL HOOD

Accountants and some qualified business coaches are trained to read the story your financial statements tell. You must seek assistance in learning what these numbers say as well as what numbers are important to measure. Your Financial Dashboard is very specific to you and your business. Most accountants are reactive by nature and are of little help in developing your dashboard but CHOOSE to focus on your numbers like they are looking in a rear view mirror. Be Proactive and hire Proactive advisors that want to help steer your financial vehicle by taking past performance and comparing specific key indicators with the results needed to achieve your goals. Use your financial statements to look forward on the road to achieving your goals to allow you to adjust your path as necessary.

Imagine if you went to the doctor sick and they looked at your vital signs from six months ago to determine how you were feeling today. NO! They take your blood pressure, check your heart rate and pulse now to see how you are now! The fact is a majority of business owners do not check their businesses' vital signs and the vital numbers you need to know on a weekly or every day basis to stay on top and be intentional in directing your resources in the right way!

PAUL HOOD, CPA

SCHEDULE A SPECIFIC TIME AND PLACE TO REVIEW YOUR NUMBERS EVERY WEEK

REAL TALK
WITH PAUL HOOD

Chet Holmes in The *Ultimate Sales Machine* says "Concentration is like a muscle, the more you exercise it the better it gets but the more interruptions you have the weaker it gets." Lack of focus is a major cause of inefficiency in the workplace. Unfortunately inefficiency is not limited to employees, owners fall victim to it just the same. When an owner is inefficient, the entire business suffers. Be diligent and specific about what, when, where, and how you are going to be successful.

Create a "system" of measuring actual results to the goals you set. A goal is half the battle. Holding yourself accountable to stick to your budget / proforma / plan is the other half.

A great place to start is have a Proactive business coach or advisor knowledgeable of your business who can hold you accountable much like how a personal trainer to get in shape is used.

Preplan! Preplan! Preplan! Are you getting the message? Success means being intentional, being intentional means preplanning, preplanning means put in your calender when you are going to review your numbers. You have done the work of defining your goals and establishing your key indicators (vital signs) of your business. Now make it a priority to review and adjust operations, marketing, and finances based upon comparing your numbers to what they need to be to each of your goals.

PAUL HOOD, CPA

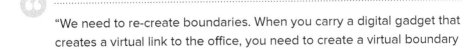

"We need to re-create boundaries. When you carry a digital gadget that creates a virtual link to the office, you need to create a virtual boundary that didn't exist before."

DANIEL GOLEMAN
(A psychologist, and New York Times bestseller of Emotional Intelligence)

SUPER MOVE #2
KNOW YOURSELF. GIVE YOURSELF ENOUGH TIME AND SPACE TO REVIEW YOUR NUMBERS CALMLY, ACCURATELY AND WITHOUT ANXIETY

REAL TALK
WITH PAUL HOOD

We are nervous and apprehensive about what we don't understand. Remember the phrase "do what you fear and the fear will disappear." Also remember this is YOUR business, YOUR life, YOUR finances. You answer only to you. No one is going to scold you or chastise you. Reviewing your numbers should be a positive thing to help you guide your business on the most engaging and joyful trip you will take with the end target being your defined goals. Do the work, measure your success with your team of Proactive advisors, and enjoy the journey. No guts no glory my friend.

Once you start this journey and the more deliberate you are the more you will begin to enjoy the process.

Imagine you have a goal to loose weight. At first you hate to step on the scale. You work the path to success and the more you stick to your plan the better the results will be.

Eventually, if you are deliberate enough and hold yourself accountable to stick to your plan, you will actively look forward to stepping on the scale!

Think about where your go to place is to not be interupted. What specific items will you need like laptop, pen, budget, etc? Plan enough time to be thorough. Do you need someone else with you. Reviewing your numbers, is just as important for your finances as the doctor reviewing your vital signs. Treat your finances like you treat your health! You are only as strong as you are honest. So be honest with yourself and your family and control your money accordingly.

PAUL HOOD, CPA

DEFINITION MAGICIAN

Anxiety: Apprehensive uneasiness or nervousness usually over an impending or anticipated ill : a state of being anxious

SUPER MOVE #3
KNOW YOUR
WEEKLY INCOME

REAL TALK
WITH PAUL HOOD

By now you have defined your financial goals which begin with gross income needed to achieve said goals. Break down your annual gross income goals into monthly and then weekly goals to achieve the annual number. This number is useless unless you compare the goal with actual results. Your financial Dashboard should report your weekly actual income to be able to compare to the income needed to achieve your goals. Your weekly income number is also needed to allow you to calculate the amount you designate to be saved or invested as part of the pay yourself first plan.

You start with long term goals but have to be able to measure it on a much shorter term. Think of target practicing with a gun. The further the target is away the greater impact a slight deviation in aming has on accuracy. The closer the target, the easier it is to adjust your aim.

People with a business need to know their weekly income because they have the ability to increase it to meet their goals. People that are employees do not have as much of an ability to immediately increase their income but believe it or not they do long term. Develope who you are because that is what you are selling. Read books insted of watching as much TV or radio. Go to coaching education siminars. Upgrade who you hang out with to gain knowledge and direction. You are enhancing your product (you), advertise your awesome self. Be the first to work (beat your boss) and the last to leave. Leadership is taken, not always given. An employee increases their worth by taking work off of the plate of their bosses. And for gosh sake if you overdeliver and aren't appreciated, get that resume out there. Be aggressive getting the best price for you and continue to overdeliver.

PAUL HOOD, CPA

"Stay focused, work hard, know your numbers, and be disciplined. If you do those things and take care of your people, the likelihood of being successful is very, very high."

MARCUS LEMONIS
(The chairman and CEO of Camping World, Good Sam Enterprises and Gander Mountain and the star of The Profit, a CNBC reality show about saving small businesses.)

SUPER MOVE #4
KNOW YOUR
WEEKLY EXPENSES

 **REAL TALK**
WITH PAUL HOOD

Once the deep dive process happens to reduce current expense amounts as much as possible, total expenses and certain key indicator expenses need to be reported on your Proactive financial Dashboard against budgeted amounts set up to guide you on your path to reaching your financial goals. For businesses, break even calculations should be constantly monitored and adjusted as your business adjusts to the path you Proactively steer down. As the ultimate goal is for your business to provide the outcome you have defined you need to guard against possible setbacks.

Other than Insurance salesmen most people are not big fans of insurance, but it is a necessary evil. I have never heard a surviving spouse or business partner, however, say I wish we had less insurance on a deceased partner. I have for sure been involved with many situations where businesses have failed because properly funded buy-sell agreements were not in place as well as spouses having to sell businesses and other assets prematurely. That being said, insurance is one of the first places we start when evaluating expenses. Knowing where your money has gone over the last 12 months helps us analyze potential areas to cut.

As a mature Proactive business person, you must take steps to Protect as you Advance. These potential savings depend on the type and terms. This Advance and Protect strategy insures that proper planning has taken place to guard against unexpected events that could derail your plan for success. Proper planning is extremely important when it comes to insurance. Independence is vital as is using SPECIALLY DESIGNED INSURANCE when possible. Generally, we are not talking about the retail types of insurance sold by most retail insurance companies. There is not much difference when considering property and casualty, workman's compensation and general liability insurance. Life, disability, and long-term care insurance however can and should have multiple benefits creating a no lose outcome. Retail providers generally have "cookie cutter" products that are not always appropriate or competitive.

A proper analysis of an appropriate product often is not centered on cost alone. Possible future tax free income, convertibility issues, reversionary possibilities, assignability issues, and dual or multiple ways to benefit are major considerations. This type of detailed analysis needs to be done with all your insurance (car, home, disability, etc.) as well as all other expences.

Check Your List

- [ ] Know All of Your Fixed Costs
- [ ] Know All of Your Variable Costs
- [ ] Know All of Your Sneaky-Easy-to-Forget-About Costs
- [ ] Buy More Insurance and Have Less Stress. It's Better to Have a Bad Day Than a Bad Life.
- [ ] Save now regardless of your debt.

"Control your expenses better than your competition. This is where you can always find the competitive advantage."

SAM WALTON
(The founder of Walmart)

DEFINITION MAGICIAN

A fixed cost is a cost that does not change with an increase or decrease in the amount of goods or services produced or sold. Fixed costs are expenses that have to be paid by a company, independent of any business activity. It is one of the two components of the total cost of running a business, along with variable cost.
Forbes

A variable cost is a corporate expense that varies with production output. Variable costs are those costs that vary depending on a company's production volume; they rise as production increases and fall as production decreases. Variable costs differ from fixed costs such as rent, advertising, insurance and office supplies, which tend to remain the same regardless of production output. Fixed costs and variable costs comprise total cost.
Forbes

AMPLE EXAMPLES OF SNEAKY COSTS

 Breakage/Errors/Refunds

 Insurance for Disasters

 Lawsuits/ Legal Bills

 Liability Insurance

 Taxes

 Theft

AMPLE EXAMPLES OF INSURANCE

 Home and Auto

 Life Insurance

 Umbrella Insurance

 Disability Insurance

 Liability Insurance

 Workman's Comp Insurance

 Long-term Care Insurance

KNOW YOUR
WEEKLY PROFIT

REAL TALK
WITH PAUL HOOD

The reason that you as a business owner show up to work everyday is to make a profit. You have defined your goals and now need to measure the net result. There are two different "profits" to measure. Gross Profit and Net Profit. Gross Profit is calculated by the difference between Total Sales less the cost to produce the product or service. Generally this Gross Profit number is also the denominator in the Breakeven calculation (sales - variable costs). Net Profit is the bottom line number taking all expenses from sales and represents the total net results of operations, manufacturing, administrative and marketing. Weekly Profit should be calculated and compared to the weekly goal setup to continue on the path of success to meet your goals. These numbers should be reported on your Proactive Financial Dashboard.

Individuals can look at their finances like net profit as well. You have income coming in, expenses necessary to live going out (fixed costs) and luxury or lifestyle expenses that typically go up as you make more income (variable costs). Profit should equal 10% of gross income or 20% of net for a diligent employee.

A good target for most businesses is 20% - 30% of sales as a net profit. If you are not at this range, an analysis to decrease expenses and/or increase prices on your product or service should be done.

PAUL HOOD, CPA

"I would rather earn 1% off 100 people's efforts than 100% of my own efforts."

JOHN D. ROCKEFELLER
(A self-made success who began working at the age of 16 to support his mother.)

DEFINITION MAGICIAN

Profit is the excess of the selling price of goods over their cost

FUN FACTS

A Healthy Profit Margin Needs to Be Between 25-30%

You Don't Make Any Profit Until You Break Even

"Profit in business comes from repeat customers, customers that boast about your project or service, and that bring friends with them."

W. EDWARDS DEMING
(Many in Japan credit Deming as one of the inspirations for what has become known as the Japanese post-war economic miracle of 1950 to 1960, when Japan rose from the ashes of war on the road to becoming the second largest economy in the world through processes partially influenced by the ideas Deming taught)

"Rule No.1: Never lose money. Rule No. 2: Never forget rule No. 1."

WARREN BUFFETT
(As of March 2017 is the second wealthiest person in the United States, and the fourth wealthiest in the world, with a total net worth of $73.3 billion)

KNOW YOUR
WEEKLY SAVINGS

REAL TALK
WITH PAUL HOOD

Business owners start businesses for various reasons including the desire to control their own time and destiny. If you work for someone else you are getting paid about 30% of what you are worth. Business owners get paid for 100% of their efforts if they choose the right path and hire the right advisors to bridge the gap of they don't know what they don't know. Even if a person owns a business, he or she is a fool if they do not diversify their current asset holdings and future income streams. Never put all your eggs in one basket. Take a percentage of sales and diversify into savings or investments. Harness the power of compound interest and or dollar cost averaging. Plan for a future where you buy back your time and have the ability to work because you want to and not because you have to. Saving out of gross instead of waiting to save out of net doubles your chances of success.

Proverbs 21:20 says "the wise man saves for the future, but the foolishman spends whatever he gets." God himself directs us to SAVE. The answer to most peoples financial issues is to save first. Even people with debt should save now because they will reduce their available funds to spend and learn to live below their means. Listen to Warren Buffett and God! Save the first of your fruits! Live on 70% - 80% of your net!

PAUL HOOD, CPA

> "Don't save what is left after spending, but spend what is left after saving."

WARREN BUFFETT
(Legendary self-made billionaire investor)

> "Too many people spend money they earned... To buy things they don't want... To impress people that they don't like."

WILL ROGERS
(A stage and motion picture actor, humorist, newspaper columnist, and social commentator)

FUN FACT

A Healthy Savings
Amount is 5%
of Your Gross
Income

Hood and Associates have a great team and put on a great business workshop. Learned about A players and gained very actionable items to immediately implement in our business.

Shaw Homes – Aaron Antis

CHOOSE THE RIGHT INVESTMENT VEHICLES AND THE RIGHT ADVISORS

REAL TALK
WITH PAUL HOOD

The decisions you make with respect to investment vehicles and who you work with as an advisor are extremely important and often involve issues the average person is not equipped to address. An advisor helps people make similar decisions hundreds of times whereas individuals have very little experience making decisions on their own. The problem becomes then which advisor is the best and can you have faith they are recommending the best investment vehicle for you or are they simply selling "cookie cutter" plans. Is it really a financial plan if everyone they meet with has the same product mix? The answer is a resounding NO!

Think of your financial assets as a professional baseball team. You need to hire a manager to get shoulder to shoulder with you to help you define what type of team you want. Your manager then would compare potential players for your team against their peers and help you hire the best. Once the team is fielded the manager continually evaluates your players against other potential players. If they perform well, he keeps them; if not, he replaces them. This analogy is relevant because most people hire a financial manager from a major brokerage house, mutual fund house, or insurance company. These managers are actually playing shortstop for you by picking investments and are not going to come to you and say the person down the road is doing better than them and fire themselves. They are asset gatherers or product salesmen.

An independent financial advisor is extremely important. This advisor will tell you if you need traditional investments, insurance products, or more nontraditional products. They will address all of your needs including trusts, wills and long-term care. They will not be the product expert they will be the plan expert. They will bring in providers of financial products and make them compete for your business on your behalf, monitor their results against their peers and fire them if they don't perform. His or her job is to make sure you know WHY you have a certain financial products and how that product plays a role in reaching your goals.

PAUL HOOD, CPA

REAL TALK
WITH PAUL HOOD

Anything you have equity in through investing your hard earned funds in is an asset including your home. Under current market conditions your home generally is an under-performing asset, is illiquid and generally is not invested in to sale. For this reason it really is not an investment. Interest rates are very low and bank mortgages are generally better funds to use than your liquid investable assets. People like to have their home paid off for the warm fuzzy feeling but the reality is that their beneficiaries are the ones that will benefit from investing liquid assets into their home.

A great way to think about what a good investment is to think of investments as minions (the little cartoon dwarves). Investments work for you to produce revenue and other minions. When you have enough minions you can buy back your time. Why would you slaughter minions to pay your house off? Your home is a cash flow item just like other expenses. Keep your house payments low and count it in the 70% - 80% of your net income limit.

PAUL HOOD, CPA

SAVINGS VEHICLE #2
ACTIVELY MANAGED PORTFOLIOS / MUTUAL FUNDS

 ### REAL TALK
WITH PAUL HOOD

Traditional stock and bond investments generally fall into two different categories, Separately Managed Accounts ("SMA") and Mutual Funds ("MF"). To be successful in investing you generally need three things - diversification, time to weather ups and downs, and professional money management. The primary driver for people to determine whether to invest in a SMA or MF is how much investable assets do they have to be able to have proper diversification. Generally unless you have at least 1 million dollars you can not get a top shelf money manager to work with you and thus have to invest in MFs.

A SMA and a MF at their source are actually the same thing and consists of a group of money managers buying and selling stocks and bonds. A SMA holds the actual stocks and bonds. A MF is a pool of funds as defined above. The primary issue with MFs are their expense (fees and fund costs), the limitations of sectored funds, and the fact you share investments with other investors which more times than not make irrational investment decisions that have a direct negative effect on you.

You should take great care in what your advisor recommends. If MFs are the investment of choice retail level funds that you have all heard of are generally much more expensive. With the correct INDEPENDENT FINANCIAL ADVISOR you can get the diversification of a MF without paying the high costs of retail investments.

There are institutional money managers that report their funds like a mutual fund but are not available to the general public thus mitigating the irrational decisions most investors make. The average person buys when the market is up and sells when it is down. Completely opposite of what you should do.

PAUL HOOD, CPA

DEFINITION MAGICIAN

A mutual fund is an investment vehicle made up of a pool of funds collected from many investors for the purpose of investing in securities such as stocks, bonds, money market instruments and similar assets. Mutual funds are operated by money managers, who invest the fund's capital and attempt to produce capital gains and income for the fund's investors. A mutual fund's portfolio is structured and maintained to match the investment objectives stated in its prospectus.

Investopedia

SAVINGS VEHICLE #3
ANNUITIES

 **REAL TALK
WITH PAUL HOOD**

Annuities simply put are an insurance version of other investments. Fixed annuities are alternatives for CD's. Variable annuities are alternatives for SMAs or MF accounts. Indexed annuities are a hybrid product allowing investors to share in investment returns if the market goes up without the downside potential of traditional stock or bond investments. Most people think of what is called a Single Premium Immediate Annuity (SPIA) when they hear the word annuity. This type of annuity is a guaranteed monthly payment for life or for a specified term but if you die early the insurance company keeps your money. Most are not this type.

When you have an insurance product you are insuring something like your life, home, car etc. Annuities offer a feature called a living benefit that insures your income. Annuity products for the right investor can produce unbeatable results. For the wrong investor they can be an absolutely terrible product. Once again an Independent Financial Advisor should be consulted. A person that works for an insurance company strangely enough may not be the best person to consult regarding whether to use an annuity.

Annuities come into play when a good planner wants to transfer, risk of losses or risk of running out of money in retirement. In the distribution phase of life risk and volatility are not your friend. For some people annuities offer a good alternative

PAUL HOOD, CPA

DEFINITION MAGICIAN

An annuity is a contractual financial product sold by financial institutions that is designed to accept and grow funds from an individual and then, upon annuitization, payout a stream of payments to the individual at a later point in time. The period of time when an annuity is being funded and before payouts begin is referred to as the accumulation phase. Once payments commence, the contract is in the annuitization phase.
Investopedia

CD = Cash Deposit

WHOLE LIFE INSURANCE

 ## REAL TALK WITH PAUL HOOD

Whole life policies are permanent life insurance policies that as long as premiums continue to be paid the policy will not lapse as opposed to term insurance which is very inexpensive and a majority of time never pays off. Whole life policies generally are not considered good investments but can offer the dual benefit of death benefit and potential tax-free retirement. Strangely enough there are times when a Whole Life policy on the joint lives of a married couple will actually outperform over-funding of a 401(k) as a retirement funding vehicle in addition to the death benefit. A competent Independent Financial Advisor can assist you in evaluating whether this product could play a positive role in your financial plan.

PAUL HOOD, CPA

DEFINITION MAGICIAN

Whole life insurance is a contract with premiums that includes insurance and investment components. The insurance component pays a predetermined amount when the insured individual dies. The investment component builds an accumulated cash value the insured individual can borrow against or withdraw. This is the most basic type of cash-value life insurance.
Investopedia

SAVINGS VEHICLE #5
INDEXED LIFE INSURANCE

DEFINITION MAGICIAN

A permanent life insurance policy that allows policyholders to tie accumulation values to a stock market index. Indexed universal life insurance policies typically contain a minimum guaranteed fixed interest rate component along with the indexed account option. Indexed policies give policyholders the security of fixed universal life insurance with the growth potential of a variable policy linked to indexed returns.

Investopedia

 REAL TALK WITH PAUL HOOD

Indexed Life Insurance is a hybrid permanent life insurance product fitting in between a whole life policy which uses non-equity investments and a Variable Life Policy that invests in equity investments like Mutual Funds. The discussion above equally applies to Indexed Life Insurance except for the potential for higher returns being tied to a stock market index for participating in market gains without the risk of loss.

Cash balance policies work based upon the idea that normally you only pay life insurance costs on the difference between the cash value and the death benefit. Therefore, the quicker you get money in the policy and the better the earnings the lower the policy actually costs.

PAUL HOOD, CPA

ROTH IRA

DEFINITION MAGICIAN

Named for Delaware Senator William Roth and established by the Taxpayer Relief Act of 1997, a Roth IRA is an individual retirement plan (a type of qualified retirement plan) that bears many similarities to the traditional IRA. The biggest distinction between the two is how they're taxed. Since traditional IRAs contributions are made with pretax dollars, you pay income tax when you withdraw the money from the account during retirement. Conversely, Roth IRAs are funded with after-tax dollars; the contributions are not tax deductible (although you may be able to take a tax credit of 10 to 50% of the contribution), depending on your income and life situation). But when you start withdrawing funds, these qualified distributions are tax free.

Investopedia

REAL TALK WITH PAUL HOOD

Roth IRA is a very limited investment vehicle as far as amounts that can be used to fund it. Simply defined money going in is not tax deductible but investment income and returns can be withdrawn at retirement income tax free.

A large portion of time in a proactively planned future, investing pretax generally outpaces a Roth IRA. Earning money on the money you have to give the government some time far off in the future is the primary contributor to the superiority of pretax investments.

For instance, if someone comes to you and said you can pay them $1,000 today or pay them $1,000 twenty years from now and also keep 80% of the earnings on that $1,000 over the twenty year term. Why would you pay now? Roths play a role but generally we recommend no more than 30% of your retirement assets into Roth. This of course depends on many factors and is based upon each individuals needs.

PAUL HOOD, CPA

SAVINGS VEHICLE #7
INVEST IN ADVERTISING (5%)

 ## REAL TALK WITH PAUL HOOD

Anything you put money into to get a return can be considered an investment. Investing in Advertising is a nontraditional "investment" and is NOT a replacement for Paying Yourself First by taking a percentage of sales to set aside in savings or investments. There are many different ways to invest in Advertising and it is vital to have a competent business or marketing coach. It is extremely important to choose the correct method to advertise based upon your budget, target audience, goals for results, type of product or service you sell among other considerations. CONSULT AN EXPERT before investing in advertising. All that being said, advertising is the gas to your money making vehicle. It doesn't do any good to have a great product or service if no one knows about it! Like a systematic savings plan, advertising needs to be consistent and often takes time to realize the results. Define who your likely buyers are and how can they be reached the most efficiently. Measure results by tracking dollars spent with results gained. Google is one of the primary methods today's customers use to make decisions. A direct strategy including optimizing how you show up on internet searches should be one of the primary focuses for most businesses.

PAUL HOOD, CPA

"The future of advertising is the Internet."

BILL GATES
(Co-founder of Microsoft)

"Half the battle is selling music, not singing it. It's the image, not what you sing."

ROD STEWART
(British rock singer and songwriter. Born and raised in London, he is of Scottish and English ancestry. Stewart is one of the best-selling music artists of all time, having sold over 100 million records worldwide.)

"Stopping advertising to save money is like stopping your watch to save time."

HENRY FORD
(Although Ford did not invent the automobile or the assembly line, he developed and manufactured the first automobile that many middle class Americans could afford.)

TRUSTS/ENTITY PLANNING

REAL TALK WITH PAUL HOOD

DEFINITION MAGICIAN

A Trust is a fiduciary relationship in which one party known as a trustor gives another party, the trustee, the write to hold title to property or assets for the benefit of a third party, the beneficiary.

Investopedia

Trusts and entity planning is a very complex area that definitely demands you have a knowledgeable advisor. An attorney is needed to draft documents but some Proactive Accountants and Financial Advisors can guide you as to what type of entity might be appropriate for you. For businesses, consideration should be given to entities such as LLC's, LLP's, General Partnerships, Corporations, S-Corporations, Sole-Proprietorships and Limited Partnerships. Trusts generally are at the individual level.

For instance, did you know the IRS does not recognize an LLC as a tax entity. You have to tell them how it will be taxed (Sole Proprietor, Partnership, Corporation). The decision on how taxed will depend upon various issues like is the activity passive, active or investment, how much profit is expected, how many owners, what benefits are anticipated, will you have employees, etc.

A trust can simply be put in place to facilitate the transfer of assets at death privately, quickly, and inexpensively. A trust can also be used to control assets from the grave to protect families from bankruptcy, lawsuits and divorce. Unearned wealth is almost always a bad thing. In other words people that inherit money they didn't earn generally do not do smart things with it. They have not developed financially to point to be able to make good decisions. A trust can protect them from inappropriate decisions. Significant planning opportunities exist from a tax avoidance, legal protection and asset protection standpoint. A Proactive Accountant and Financial Advisor should be consulted.

PAUL HOOD, CPA

SAVINGS VEHICLE #9
ADVISORS

 ## REAL TALK
WITH PAUL HOOD

As stated earlier, the scariest thing is you do not know what you do not know. One of the most important things you can do is surround yourself with a team of Independent Advisors. Independence simply means your interest come first above the advisors and above any company the advisor might work for or represent. The funds you pay an advisor should return to you ten fold at a minimum. Clearly you should consider these funds as an investment. As a matter of fact, if you choose the correct team of advisors, this investment will be the most fruitful one you ever make. Your team will guide you and educate you in areas you wish you would have learned in college. Practical and relevant advice to help you steer your business through the use of a Proactive Financial Dashboard includes guidance on hiring, marketing, entity planning, financial investments, mitigating taxes, entity planning, and legal protection.

If possible you want to consult with someone who is considered a fiduciary to you. A fiduciary is someone who has a moral and legal obligation to put your interests first. When a person can be sued for not putting your interests above themselves and the company they represent, they tend to be more of a "you first" advisor.

PAUL HOOD, CPA

Check Your List:
The Coaches & Advisors Everyone Needs

- ☐ Attorney
- ☐ Accountant
- ☐ Consultant/Coach
- ☐ Financial Planner

"With no feedback, no coaching, there's just no way to improve."

BILL GATES
(Co-founder of Microsoft)

"No one lives long enough to learn everything they need to learn starting from scratch. To be successful, we absolutely, positively have to find people who have already paid the price to learn the things that we need to learn to achieve our goals."

BRIAN TRACY
(Is an American motivational public speaker and self-development author)

"Best advice I ever got. The advice that sticks out I got from John Doerr, who in 2001 said, "My advice to you is to have a coach." The coach he said I should have is Bill Campbell. I initially resented the advice, because after all, I was a CEO. I was pretty experienced. Why would I need a coach? Am I doing something wrong? My argument was, How could a coach advise me if I'm the best person in the world at this? But that's not what a coach does. The coach doesn't have to play the sport as well as you do. They have to watch you and get you to be your best. In the business context a coach is not a repetitious coach. A coach is somebody who looks at something with another set of eyes, describes it to you in [his] words, and discusses how to approach the problem.

Once I realized I could trust him and that he could help me with perspective, I decided this was a great idea. When there is [a] business conflict you tend to get rat-holed into it. [Bill's] general advice has been to rise one step higher, above the person on the other side of the table, and to take the long view. He'll say, "You're letting it bother you. Don't.""

ERIC SCHMIDT
(Former CEO of Google)

When I started my business, I was determined to work with professionals to have the best start possible. Working with Hood & Associates was a no-brainer. Friendly staff always ready to help with whatever you need, a proven system to properly plan and execute, and an amazing owner who wants his clients to win. Their professionalism is apparent in all that they do. I appreciate all of the help they have given me and my business and look forward to a continued relationship.

Turley-Schenck Innovations, LLC - Rance Turley

KNOW HOW TO ACCURATELY PRICE YOUR PRODUCTS AND SERVICES

REAL TALK WITH PAUL HOOD

Your business is by you, for you, and to benefit you. Define what activities you enjoy, what type of person you want to work with, how much money your efforts are worth, and how long you want to do it. Create enough revenue to pay others to do what you don't want to do and what is not the best use of your time. Why spend the only time you have doing things you don't like, working with people you don't like or not being paid what you desire? Throughout this book we have discussed the methodology of breaking down your numbers into the sales you need to live the life you want. You start with the end in mind by defining the net income needed to meet your needs. Then calculating your fixed and variable costs to determine the amount of sales you need. Most people almost guess how to price their products. You need to mathematically determine what your price needs to be to meet your needs. Shop your competition, create an environment that makes people want to buy from you, determine if you compete on price or luxury experience and constantly evaluate areas to be able to overdeliver to maximize the price you can charge.

"You know that you've found market price when buyers complain, but still pay."

PAUL GRAHAM
(An English computer scientist, entrepreneur, venture capitalist, author, and blogger)

"When I was 5 years old, my mother always told me that happiness was the key to life. When I went to school, they asked me what I wanted to be when I grew up. I wrote down 'happy'. They told me I didn't understand the assignment, and I told them they didn't understand life."

JOHN LENNON
(Legendary musician and member of The Beatles)

BUILD THE BUSINESS MODEL TO SERVICE Y

Define how many customers you need to break-even:

Define how many customers you need per week to achieve your F6 lifestyle:

What does it cost on an annual basis t achieve your faith goals?

What does it cost on an annual basis t achieve your family goals?

What does it cost on an annual basis t achieve your friendship goals?

What does it cost on an annual basis t achieve your fitness goals?

What does it cost on an annual basis t achieve your fun?

What does it cost on an annual basis t achieve your financial goals?

> "Financial peace isn't the acquisition of stuff. It's learning to live on less than you make, so you can give money back and have money to invest. You can't win until you do this."

DAVE RAMSEY
(National talk show and New York Times best-selling author)

DECIDE WHAT PRICE POINT AND PRODUCT CLASS YOU ARE

> "Brand is just a perception, and perception will match reality over time. Sometimes it will be ahead, other times it will be behind. But brand is simply a collective impression some have about a product."

ELON MUSK
(Musk is the founder, CEO, and CTO of SpaceX; a co-founder, a Series A investor, CEO, and product architect of Tesla Inc.; co-chairman of OpenAI; founder and CEO of Neuralink. He was previously co-founder and chairman of SolarCity; co-founder of Zip2; and founder of X.com, which merged with Confinity and took the name PayPal.)

AMPLE EXAMPLE

Exclusive = Lamborghini

Luxury = Mercedes

Value Focused = Honda

Inexpensive = The 1989 Ford Escort Clay Clark once drove

AMPLE EXAMPLE

Exclusive = Godiva Chocolate

Luxury = See's Candy

Value Focused = Dove Chocolate

Inexpensive = Hershey's Chocolate Bar

 REAL TALK WITH PAUL HOOD

You can't be everything to everyone. Your method of marketing, your store / office atmosphere, your pricing, your packaging, etc. are all determined to meet your customers in the market place based upon the market you serve. An example of miss-matched markets & markets served is the mouse trap that was developed to look very high-end fancy and was actually cost comparable to cheap traps. This fancy trap failed because consumers hated to throw it away so they chose the cheap trap instead. Regardless of the product market you strive for, your numbers at the bottom line should play a large role in determining what you charge. Determine the minimum price you need to cover your fixed and variable costs to get your desired net profit. Don't Guess! Calculate!

HOW TO PRICE YOUR PRODUCTS OR SERVICES

Fixed Costs Needed to Deliver the Product or Service:

_____

Marketing Costs Needed to Deliver the Product or Service:

_____

Variable Costs Needed to Deliver the Product or Service:

_____

25% - 30% Profit Margin:

_____

"The buyer is entitled to a bargain. The seller is entitled to a profit. So there is a fine margin in between where the price is right. I have found this to be true to this day whether dealing in paper hats, winter underwear or hotels."

CONRAD HILTON
(Self-made hotelier and the founder of the Hilton Hotels chain.)

"What you don't know will hurt you."

JIM ROHN
(Best-selling author and renowned sales trainer)

MYSTERY SHOPPING YOUR COMPETITION

What does competitor A charge for the products and services that you deliver?

_____

What does competitor B charge for the products and services that you deliver?

_____

What does competitor C charge for the products and services that you deliver?

_____

REAL TALK WITH PAUL HOOD

Price your product to maximize profitability to benefit you. You are not a non profit. You provide value and put in extra effort. You should be rewarded for it. Price your products high enough where consumers will still even if they complain about it. Competition along with supply and demand determine your pricing... not your feelings. If the price you determine you need is more than the competition you have to either cut costs to lower price or over deliver the experience, packaging, guarantee or follow through!

THE APPROPRIATE PROFIT MARGIN

WHETHER YOU RAISE PRICES OR NOT INFLATION IS DEVALUING YOUR CURRENCY

REAL TALK WITH PAUL HOOD

A vast majority of businesses appear to be almost embarrassed about the price of their products or services. Why be in business if you can not achieve your financial goals. Your business's primary purpose is to PAY YOU! Establish your financial goals and back into the sales price you need to achieve your goals. Always have a systematic process of raising the price of your products or services to keep pace with inflation at a minimum. Shop your competition, offer superior product or service, create raving fans out of your customers and you will not have to focus on the price of your product from a negative standpoint. Inflation causes prices to go up on your supplies, employee pay, shipping, and advertising. You have to keep the calculations of your costs current to properly price your product or service. At a minimum increase your price 3% annually to stay at pace with the average inflation.

PAUL HOOD, CPA

"Pigs get fat, hogs get butchered."

DOCTOR ZOELLNER
(CEO of ThriveTimeShow.com, the founder of DrZoellner.com, member of original BankRegent.com investment team, founder of DRZzzs.com, founder of Z66AA.com, etc...)

"Because Government does not have the ability to control their spending and they do have the ability to print unlimited amount of fiat currency whenever the heck they want your money will lose 2% to 3% of its' value every year."

CLAY TIBERIUS CLARK
(Host of the ThriveTimeShow.com, writer for Forbes, former U.S. SBA Entrepreneur of the Year, father of 5 human kids, founder of EpicPhotos.com, founder of MakeYourLifeEpic.com, founder of ThriveTimeShow.com, former owner of Party Perfect (now known as PartyProRents.com, co-founder of EITRLounge.com, etc.)

DEFINITION MAGICIAN

The general increase in prices and fall in the purchasing value of money. Inflation is the rate at which the general level of prices for goods and services is rising and, consequently, the purchasing power of currency is falling. Central banks attempt to limit inflation, and avoid deflation, in order to keep the economy running smoothly.
Investopedia

We use Hood and Associates for all our tax, investment and audit work, they are fantastic to work with and extremely knowledgeable. We are very satisfied with their services. I would highly recommend Paul and his staff.

Hilliary Communications Group - Dean Pennello

KNOW THE TRUE COST OF EMPLOYEES

"I noticed that the dynamic range between what an average person could accomplish and what the best person could accomplish was 50 or 100 to 1. Given that, you're well advised to go after the cream of the cream... A small team of A+ players can run circles around a giant team of B and C players."

STEVE JOBS

Salary or Hourly Cost

Office Space Cost

Insurance Cost

Management Layer Costs

Social Security Cost

C-Player Costs (Repelling Business)

Workmen's Compensation (1% to 2%)

Employee Theft (Intentional or Wasted time)

Training Time

Non-Productive Time (Vacation/Sick)

Top 20% (A-Players)

"When people differentiation is real, the top 20 percent of employees are showered with bonuses, stock options, praise, love, training, and a variety of rewards to their pocketbooks and souls. There can be no mistaking the stars at a company that differentiates. They are the best and are treated that way."

Middle 70% (B-Players)

"The middle 70 percent are managed differently. This group of people is enormously valuable to any company; you simply cannot function without their skills, energy, and commitment. After all, they are the majority of your employees. And that's the major challenge, and risk, in 20-70-10—keeping the middle 70 engaged and motivated.

That's why so much of managing the middle 70 is about training, positive feedback, and thoughtful goal setting. If individuals in this group have particular promise, they should be moved around among businesses and functions to increase their experience and knowledge and to test their leadership skills.

To be clear, managing the middle 70 is not about keeping people out of the bottom 10. It is not about saving poor performers. That would be a bad investment decision. Rather, differentiation is about managers looking at the middle 70, identifying people with potential to move up, and cultivating them. But everyone in the middle 70 needs to be motivated and made to feel as if they truly belong. You do not want to lose the vast majority of your middle 70—you want to improve them."

Bottom 10% (C-Players)

"As for the bottom 10 percent in differentiation, there is no sugar coating this—they have to go. That's more easily said than done; It's awful to fire people—I even hate that word. But if you have a candid organization with clear performance expectations and a performance evaluation process—a big if, obviously, but that should be everyone's goal—then people in the bottom 10 percent generally know who they are. When you tell them, they usually leave before you ask them to."

JACK WELCH
(The former CEO of GE who grew up the company by 400% during his tenure)

REAL TALK
WITH PAUL HOOD

The largest expense of a lot of businesses is their payroll. It is often the hardest to quantify. It isn't simply the pay rate, it also includes such things as taxes, insurance, office space, office supplies, cost of wasted time, cost of inefficiencies, training, theft, and attitude and personality causing loss of business. Also as your staff grows you will need more managers because unfortunately most employees have to be watched and pushed like kindergardeners.

On average one manager is needed for every 7 employees and a good estimate for true employee cost is 2 times their pay rate. Unfortunately even though employee cost is often the largest expense of a lot of businesses, most owners are the weakest at managing this cost. Emotion, loyalty, fear, and business relationship issues cloud making good employee decisions. If you had a copy machine that worked half the time and cost you more than it is worth , you would not hesitate to replace it. But a person has feelings and may be married to your cousin.

People have lives and we naturally care about how our activities effect them. This is your business, your money, your time and you have to make tough decisions.

Most of the time people are overachievers or underperformers pureley based on choices they have made and continue to make. It is not your fault they choose to slack off and underperform. Your business is only as strong as your weakest employee.

Shake off the entitlement attitude that poisons most businesses. Tough love is best for you, them and your business. Remember, also slothfullness breeds slothfullness and great attitude and work ethic breed the same among other employees. Get rid of the disease of sub par employees that is making your business sick!

Think of your business as a professional football team which ALWAYS strives to get the best players possible at every position. Constantly be looking to hire better payers and evaluate if you have the wrong players in the wrong position. If your quarterback leaves you should already have the backup ready to go into the game. The worst thing owners do is to wait to find or have replacements until someone leaves. You end up wasting time on interviews to hire the best of the worst. There is a system to continually be in the hiring and upgrading mind state of operating your business.

DEVELOPING YOUR ACCOUNTING ROUTINES

REAL TALK
WITH PAUL HOOD

Chet Holmes in The Ultimate Sales Machine says "people respect what you inspect". Do you respect your goals enough to be Proactive? To hire advisors that are Proactive? To know your strengths and weaknesses and ask for help? To seek guidance to be able to read the story your accounting tells you? To use your numbers to look forward like a vehicle dashboard and not just as a rear-view mirror? To have real time accounting so you can at any time compare actual to planned? To be held accountable to doing what it takes to reach your financial goals? To pay yourself first like the top 10% of people do instead of like the last(or bottom) 90%? Take the time to plan for success, measure your actual results against your plan, modify your actions to stay on track to reach your goals!!

Once you have put the time in to know where your money is going, where you want it to go and what income numbers you need to reach your goals, you have to preplan when you are going to complete and evaluate your results. Weekly you should look at your key performance indicators to see if you are on track. These numbers generally are the 5 - 10 most important income and expense items that can make or break you. Examples would be bank balance, unit sales, calls made, new sales, payroll as a percentage of sales, etc. A more extensive look at all numbers is often done more on a monthly basis

PAUL HOOD, CPA

Check Your List

☐ On-Going Accounting Routines

☐ Develop a Set Place to Handle Your Accounting

☐ Develop a Set Time to Handle Your Accounting

☐ Develop an Organization System for Your Accounting

☐ Develop the Habit of Touching It Once

☐ Develop a Set Time for Reconciling Your Bank Accounts

☐ The Importance of Paying Your Bills Electronically
(Avoid the Bag of Receipts Game)

☐ Analyze Your Financial Dashboard

☐ Schedule a Standing Monthly Meeting with Your Accountant

☐ Schedule someone to do accounting with you

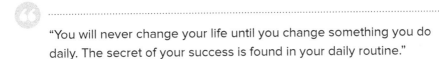

"You will never change your life until you change something you do daily. The secret of your success is found in your daily routine."

JOHN MAXWELL
(Best-selling author of The 21 Irrefutable Laws of Leadership)

"Long term success is a direct result of what you achieve everyday. Goals provide your daily routine."

RICK PITINO
(Pitino holds the distinction of being the only men's coach in history to lead two different schools to an NCAA Championship (Kentucky and Louisville). He is also the only coach to lead three different schools (Providence, Kentucky, and Louisville) to a Final Four. Pitino is one of only four coaches in NCAA history (along with Dean Smith, Mike Krzyzewski and Jim Boeheim) to take his school to the Final Four in four separate decades, one of only three coaches (along with Roy Williams and Jack Gardner) to have led two different programs to at least two Final Fours each, and one of only two coaches (along with Williams) to have led two different programs to at least three Final Fours each.)

"The secret of success is to do the common things uncommonly well."

JOHN D. ROCKEFELLER
(A self-made man who went on to become the world's wealthiest man during his lifetime)

"A daily routine built on good habits and disciplines separates the most successful among us from everyone else. The routine is exceptionally powerful."

DARREN HARDY
(Author, keynote speaker, advisor, and former publisher of SUCCESS magazine. Hardy is a New York Times best-selling author who wrote The Entrepreneur Roller Coaster and The Compound Effect)

REAL TALK WITH PAUL HOOD

In order to be able to adjust and change directions to continually enhance profitablility, you have to be able to measure actual verses planned. STOP and step out of your business in a preplanned time, method, and location to do your accounting routines. Most businesses relegate their accounting to be the last thing done. Often only doing accounting last minute for banking or taxes. If you don't preplan and have a deliberate attitude towards performing those tasks, how do you know you are on the right path financially? How do you know if you are just doing the wrong thing over and over? Victory is normally not just what you achieve in the future. The daily victories from staying faithful to your plan determine future victory, by preplanning, establishing goals and a measuring system you determine your future victory. Take luck out of the equation and replace it with intentional decisions.

AVOID THESE CASH FLOW KILLERS

REAL TALK
WITH PAUL HOOD

You must decide if your business is there to be a financial cash cow for you and your loved ones or a not-for-profit entity providing services at below market prices and allowing your employees to take advantage of you. To be in business for profit you must be deliberate in streamlining operations, in maximizing benefits received for amounts paid out, in paying yourself first, and in holding employees accountable. You are the captain and the results, good or bad, are 100% your responsibility. Success or failure will be because of you. You now have been educated on practical processes and steps to take control of the financial side of your business and life. If you completely and consistently execute the things we have discussed your success is limited only by your desire and vision.

Cash is king in business, but is often what causes the most stress. Clients say all the time, "My financials show I made money but I have NO CASH." A proactive business owner does a cash flow statement which explains where their cash went in relation to Net profit or loss. Just producing revenue is not enough, a business has to be agressive in converting sales / revenue into cash as well as plugging "cash leaks" on the expense side.

PAUL HOOD, CPA

DEFINITION MAGICIAN

Cash flow is the net amount of cash and cash-equivalents moving into and out of a business. Positive cash flow indicates that a company's liquid assets are increasing, enabling it to settle debts, reinvest in its business, return money to shareholders, pay expenses and provide a buffer against future financial challenges. Negative cash flow indicates that a company's liquid assets are decreasing. Net cash flow is distinguished from net income, which includes accounts receivable and other items for which payment has not actually been received. Cash flow is used to assess the quality of a company's income, that is, how liquid it is, which can indicate whether the company is positioned to remain solvent.
Investopedia

To NOT Do List

☐ Failing to Collect from Customers

☐ Failing to Fire Poor Performing Employees

☐ Invoicing Your Clients (When You Could Collect Payment Upfront)

☐ Casually Tracking of Inventory

☐ Casually Tracking of Expenses

☐ Casually Tracking of Accounts Payable

"Every right implies a responsibility; Every opportunity, an obligation, Every possession, a duty."

JOHN D. ROCKEFELLER
(The world's wealthiest man during his lifetime)

"A friendship founded on business is better than a business founded on friendship."

JOHN D. ROCKEFELLER
(At the age of 29 (1866), William Rockefeller Jr., John's brother, built another refinery in Cleveland and brought John into the partnership. In 1867, Henry M. Flagler became a partner, and the firm of Rockefeller, Andrews & Flagler was established. By 1868, with Rockefeller continuing practices of borrowing and reinvesting profits, controlling costs, and using refineries' waste, the company owned two Cleveland refineries and a marketing subsidiary in New York; it was the largest oil refinery in the world.)

"Do not many of us who fail to achieve big things... fail because we lack concentration--the art of concentrating the mind on the thing to be done at the proper time and to the exclusion of everything else?"

JOHN D. ROCKEFELLER
(The world's wealthiest man during his lifetime. In September 1855, when Rockefeller was sixteen, he got his first job as an assistant bookkeeper working for a small produce commission firm called Hewitt & Tuttle.)

SELF EVALUATION TIME

RATE YOURSELF ON A SCALE OF 1 TO 10, WITH 10 BEING THE HIGHEST IN THE FOLLOWING AREAS:

SUPER MOVE #1 – Your Accounting Must Be Viewed As Your Front Dash Board Not Your Rear View Mirror

1 2 3 4 5 6 7 8 9 10

SUPER MOVE #2 – Casualness Causes Casualties

1 2 3 4 5 6 7 8 9 10

SUPER MOVE #3 – AUTO-mate Your Success

1 2 3 4 5 6 7 8 9 10

SUPER MOVE #4 – Develop Clear Goals for Your Financial Future

1 2 3 4 5 6 7 8 9 10

SUPER MOVE #5 – Learning How to Read Your Financial DASHBOARD

1 2 3 4 5 6 7 8 9 10

SUPER MOVE #6 – Choose the Right Investment Vehicle

1 2 3 4 5 6 7 8 9 10

SUPER MOVE #7 – Know How to Accurately Price Your Products and Services

1 2 3 4 5 6 7 8 9 10

SUPER MOVE #8 – Know the True Cost of Employees

1 2 3 4 5 6 7 8 9 10

SUPER MOVE #9 – Developing Your Accounting Routines

1 2 3 4 5 6 7 8 9 10

SUPER MOVE #10 – Avoid These Cash Flow Killers

1 2 3 4 5 6 7 8 9 10

ACTION ITEMS

1. Pass on what you've learned by writing a Google Review. Type in "HoodCPAs" and write that review today!

2. Don't miss a radio show or podcast. Subscribe on iTunes at ThriveTimeShow.com.

3. Go to HoodCPAs.com to schedule your one hour consultation to help you save more, keep more. and protect more.

WANT MORE?

Check out the Ultimate Textbook for Starting, Running & Growing Your Own Business!

Start Here

NEVER before has entrepreneurship been delivered in an UNFILTERED, real and raw way... Until now. This book is NOT for people that want a politically correct and silver-lined happy-go-lucky view of entrepreneurship. That's crap. Supported by case studies and testimonials from entrepreneurs that have grown their businesses all over the planet using these best practice systems, former U.S. Small Business Administration Entrepreneur of the Year, Clay Clark, shares the specific action steps for successful business systems, hilarious stories from situations that every entrepreneur faces, and entrepreneurship factoids that are guaranteed to blow your mind.

Invite a Friend to Join You at the World's Best 2-Day Intensive Business Workshop

Get specific and practical training on how to grow your business

www.ThriveTimeShow.com

CPSIA information can be obtained
at www.ICGtesting.com
Printed in the USA
FSHW011113280620

9 780999 864944